31 Kings

Mental Health Game

By
Derrick Drakeford, Ph.D.

Copyright © 2022 Drakeford, Scott, & Associates, LLC
Durham, NC
All Rights Reserved.

Dedication

This book is dedicated to anyone who has ever been paralyzed by fear, anxiety, or panic. You are not alone. Though it can be scary, moving through the fear, anxiety, or panic can help anyone see life in a new dimension and better appreciate the power of your mind. Our bodies need healthy food and daily exercise to be strong. Our souls need spiritual food for inner peace and faith even in the midst of turmoil. Likewise, our <u>minds, which are often overlooked</u>, need healthy controlled thoughts. Our thoughts and feelings are a byproduct of what we see, read, think, listen to, and believe. In this book, my hope is for the reader to develop their own personal daily game to live in mental peace every day.

Contents

Introduction "Keep Going"

Exercise

So... I'm jogging today working on my long distance running time because I have a race coming up in less than a month. There is something about running a marathon that motivates me to prepare for the race. The group energy and collective motivation of other runners and the drive to push yourself to be better inspires me at marathons. Life is not a sprint it is made up of small daily decisions and routines. Artist Nispsey Hustle said "even in trying times like now, it's like the world is in panic, but we gotta keep going. **The marathon continues."** [1]

---

[1] Photo Credit: Derrick Drakeford Cooper Bridge Marathon 2022

Like running there are so many habits that I need to form that I wish I looked at in the same ways that I look at exercise in preparation for a race. Something about making it a competition or a game gives me a little extra push of motivation.

Today as I began to jog, my left hip started piercing in pain from a former repetitive motion injury. Feeling this pain always takes me back to 2020. Two years ago, I got into gardening and had a cubic ton of wood chips dropped off on my front driveway. It took 8 months and thousands of individual shovels to finally move all these chips to my future garden location. Shortly after my left hip was almost immovable and throbbed with pain after every step. I went to a physical therapist to explain my injury and walked the doctor through my shoveling motion. She helped me to learn that the real problem in my motion was that in my haste to get the work done, I never switched hands and thus kept applying pressure to the same hip every time repetitively. My problem wasn't the work itself, it was my lack of working consciously and thinking about switching hands to maintain physical balance that resulted in pain later on. If I was consciously thinking about my work, I would have regularly alternated sides to preserve my body. But I was so mission driven and mindlessly working that I worked my body out of alignment.

This moment with the doctor made me think of how many other areas of my life or my health were hurting due to not being balanced. Like my physical body, my mind and my spirit can also cause me pain when out of balance.

I was brought back to the present with the thought that I need to keep running. As I was jogging the 1st mile, my left hip was screaming in pain after each step. But as I ran through the pain, my hip suddenly warmed up and the pain became more bearable until it eventually disappeared. Then my left calf began to hurt, so I slowed down and jogged with an apparent limp. As I ran around the corner of the sidewalk near a streetlight with a line of cars stopped preparing to make a left turn, I heard some screaming in the distance. Someone shouted, "Keep Going!" I looked up and saw a middle aged African American woman with her arm out the window cheering me on. She said, "Keep going, You got this!" I pumped my fist back to her in thanks and suddenly my calf stopped hurting and I picked up speed. Since I now had an entire audience of cars, I kicked it into overdrive and sprinted down the sidewalk. I looked like a middle aged Usan Bolt with locks. After I turned off the street, I kept going fast without the audience. I could even hear in my mind's ear the lady from the red truck screaming," Keep going, You got this!".

I realized that I could choose to keep hearing her words of encouragement in my mind instead of replacing them with my complaints and pains. Just like the pupil of an eye gets larger when it focuses on an object, our mind's eye gets larger when we consciously choose to focus on a thought. Whether negative or positive, when we focus on a thought, it becomes larger in our mind. Our minds are so powerful that what we choose to focus on can impact our health. When I choose to focus on pain or a future worry, my heart starts racing and I can feel my breath getting shorter. All from what I have chosen to think about. But sometimes I forget that I even have the power to choose and I let my mind run wild on its own from thought to thought and fear to fear until it becomes all consuming.

This day I chose to focus my mind on the encouraging words of a stranger. Her words of "Keep Going! You Can Do it" became my mental soundtrack. When I got back home and checked out my jogging time on my mobile app, it was the best I had run in the past two years. The stranger in the truck became the soundtrack in my head and it helped me to exceed my physical exercise goal for the day. In our culture of silence around mental health, many find it easier to encourage a stranger's (or friend's) physical health over their own mental health. In many faith cultures, it's easier to approach a stranger about their spiritual health than their mental health. In many ways, the purpose of this book is to give to the reader what this stranger in the truck gave me – a positive mental soundtrack. Another title for this book could be "Keep Going", but as you find out later in the book, 31 Kings fits better.

Why this book

What is Mental Health?
Ranna Parekh, M.D., M.P.H. in a review published by the American Psychiatric Association[2] defines mental health as;

> Mental *Health*...involves effective functioning in <u>daily</u> activities resulting in:
> - Productive activities (work, school, caregiving).
> - Healthy relationships.
> - Ability to adapt to change and cope with adversity.

What is Mental Illness?
Dr. Parekh goes on to define mental illness as;

> - Significant changes in thinking, emotion and/or behavior.
> - Distress and/or problems functioning in social, work or family activities.

Self-Help
Dr. Parekh notes there are ways we can improve our own mental health, he suggests;

> Self-help and support can be very important to an individual's coping, recovery, and wellbeing. <u>Lifestyle changes, such as good nutrition, exercise, and adequate sleep can support mental health and recovery.</u> Many people who have a mental illness do not want to talk about it. But mental illness is

---

[2] https://www.psychiatry.org/patients-families/what-is-mental-illness

nothing to be ashamed of! It is a medical condition, just like heart disease or diabetes. And mental health conditions are treatable.

The Shadow of Silence

There is a shadow of silence around the topic of mental health. This silence is so loud that people who are struggling with their own mental health are not acknowledging it until the mind or body gives us an alarm. For me it was undercurrents of anxiety and fear that I left unattended, which ultimately swelled into a panic attack. Later in this book, I will discuss more about my personal battle for mental territory with panic and anxiety. For other readers, mental health may manifest as depression, moodiness, isolation or a host of other manifestations.

Research finds, *"people are grappling with our own shadow of addressing the overwhelming and insidious shadow of mental health systems to overcome the culture of silence around this issue.*[3] Due to the culture of silence, studies find many *"people of color do not receive adequate treatment for mental health problems."*[4]

---

[3] Kemble, R. (2014). The intolerable taboo of mental illness. *Social Alternatives, 33*(3), 20-23.

[4] Alvidrez, J., Snowden, L. R., & Kaiser, D. M. (2008). The experience of stigma among Black mental health consumers. *Journal of Health Care for the Poor and Underserved, 19*(3), 874-

> "the helper" less apt to ask for "help" themselves

I include myself in this category of people who let shame prevent them from seeking and maintaining daily mental health supportive activities. I felt ashamed to have a mental health challenge. In my work with nonprofit directors and social enterprise CEOs, I've found those of us who give, serve, teach, counsel, etc. are often positioned as "the helper" and are less apt to ask for "help" themselves. Therefore, our mental health slowly degrades day by day under a shadow of silence.

For some of us, like me we start a healthy mental health practice like meditation, prayer, therapy, or a gratitude journal and then lack another person to encourage us to "keep going". At the same time, we are hyper focused on telling those we serve to "keep going". In this book, it is my hope that the people who are "helpers" develop their own mental health game to self-motivate and to keep going.

Reclaiming My Mind
This book is for servant leaders who sometimes let their attention on personal mental health fall to the bottom of their list of priorities. Here we look at mental health as a daily game. The objective is to reclaim the mental space that has been stolen by social media apps, television news anchors, or that toxic friend who keeps speaking doubt into your mind. In many ways, this is akin to Congresswoman Maxine Waters saying "reclaiming my

time"… The goal of the book is for the reader to reclaim their mind.

For those who don't know Congresswoman Maxine Waters, she did not let Treasury Secretary Steve Mnuchin waste a moment of her time when he tried to stonewall her during the House Financial Services Committee hearing. Instead of answering questions about President Donald Trump's financial ties to Russia, Mnuchin replied to one of her questions by complimenting her. In response, Walters interrupted Mnuchin using the phrase "reclaiming my time" to curtail his effort to dodge the question. "We don't want to take my time up with how great I am," she said. Nevertheless, that didn't stop Mnuchin from his attempt to derail the conversation. Each time that he tried it, Waters pressed him to give direct answers to her questions, repeating the "reclaiming my time" refrain. At one point, she told him, "You're on my time and I can reclaim it."

[5]

Every thought we entertain in our minds occupies mental space. We have to understand similarly these thoughts are "on your time and you can reclaim it". Financial stress, doubt, and negative thoughts about your future can all be reclaimed and replaced in an instant through consciously controlling your thoughts, like a game. Through gamification, we challenge ourselves to be mindful in caring deeply about our minds and intentionally focusing on loving our minds to health through small daily routines. In many ways, this book could be titled "Reclaiming My Mind" in honor of the powerful moment Congresswoman Maxine Waters exemplified. But as you will find out later in the book, 31 Kings fits better.

Replacing Mental Fear and Worry with Truth
In Luke 12:25, the Bible reads," Who of you by worrying can add a single hour to your life." Many times we worry because our minds are stuck in the past or future and we have no control of either. This book is designed to help readers cultivate personal strategies to deal with temporary thoughts of fear and consciously replace them with positive thoughts. In Philippians 4:8, the Bible reads "Finally, brothers and sisters, whatever is true, whatever is noble, whatever is right, whatever is pure, whatever is lovely, whatever is admirable—if anything is excellent or praiseworthy—think about such things". The 'such things' here are really 'true thoughts based in reality'. Often we worry about things that are not true, have not happened, and are not based in reality. So we should think about "true" things, that are noble, right and pure.

This book gives the reader a practical game-like method to develop daily habits to meditate and think about "true" things that make the mind healthy and at peace. In many ways, this book could be called "Think about True Things". But as you will find out later in the book, 31 Kings fits better.

Limitations

This book is not the end all be all of mental health. My background is in Education, specifically Culture, Curriculum, and Change, not therapy. This book is not an attempt to shrink you or therapize you. This book is a gamified curriculum developed from grounded theory, autoethnography, and literature. I value the important work of mental health professionals, and I don't claim to be one. Understanding the theory and literature is important for mental health practitioners. I don't know all mental health theories nor attempt to argue here that my research supplants existing theory and practice. As a consumer and reader, sometimes I just want to hear someone's personal story of how they found out how to better heal their minds through practical steps. That is what this book is: my story of healing my own mind.

The Science of Daily Lifestyle Changes

In the article, *Chronic inflammation in the etiology of disease across the lifespan[6],* the study found: chronic mental health issues such as depression can now be tracked and measured as inflammation in the body. With this new understanding, we see depression as the result of the mind and body thinking it is constantly under attack, which raises levels of inflammation in the body. This hyper-defense-mode is catalyzed by poor diet, sleep deprivation, lack of exposure to the sun, gut health, and environmental stressors (like poverty, racism, sexism, isolation, remote worker lifestyle, etc.).

---

[6] https://www.nature.com/articles/s41591-019-0675-0

The Etiology of Disease: Diagram

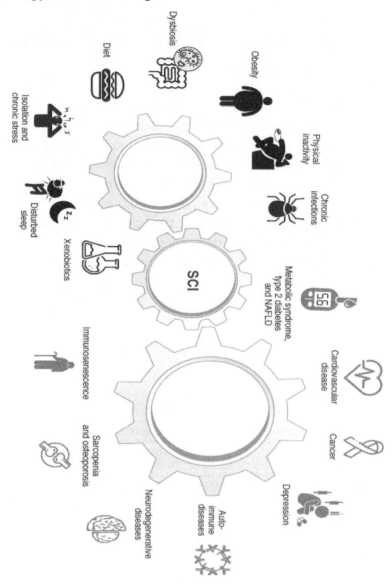

The article also points to solutions. The science finds the same self-help mental illness recovery solutions prescribed by Ranna Parekh,M.D., M.P.H. and the American Psychiatric Association: "Lifestyle changes, such as good nutrition, exercise, and adequate sleep" also prevent mental illness and inflammation in the body.

[7]The Science of Gamification

Research finds "the term 'gamification' is generally used to denote the application of gaming mechanisms in non-gaming environments with the aim of enhancing the processes enacted and experienced by those involved."[8] Here we use gamification to teach daily "Lifestyle changes, such as good nutrition, exercise, and adequate sleep."

The 31 Kings Mental Health Game uses the science of gamification to help users track and achieve daily personal physical, mental, and spiritual health goals, such as (diet, stress, sleep, exposure to the sun, gut health, etc.).

---

[7] MS Word 2020 clipart
[8] Caponetto, I., Earp, J., & Ott, M. (2014, October). Gamification and education: A literature review. In *European Conference on Games Based Learning* (Vol. 1, p. 50). Academic Conferences International Limited.

The Gamified Solution to Etiology of Disease: Diagram

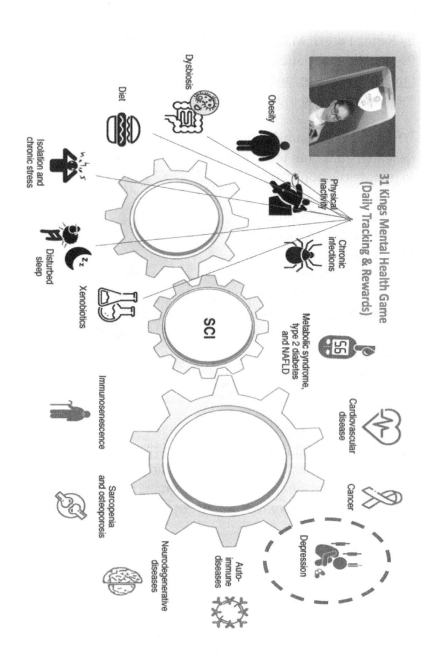

To better understand how to approach playing the 31 Kings Mental Health Game, for me, it was important to intentionally adopt a three-dimensional view of my life. I view mental health as being intimately tied and connected to the 1) mental 2) physical and 3) spiritual parts of myself. In the book Inner Engineering by Sadhguru, the author describes these three dimensions as,

> "the three fundamental sheaths (coverings), or layers of identity that every human being is conscious of. Accordingly, it is divided into three sections; Body, Mind and Energy." (Sadhguru 2016, p.87)

Like Sadhguru, three layers of identity can be seen in other texts from around the world which point to a three-dimensional view of self. For me, I began to understand this three-dimensional view of life when I chose to read the Dalai Lama while being forced to read European and African American male philosophers as a freshman in college at Bethune-Cookman University in Daytona Beach, Florida.

My Background on 3D View of Self

When I landed in Daytona Beach, Florida to begin my freshman year at Bethune-Cookman College, I was introduced to classical readings in philosophy in a textbook entitled Introduction to Great Books. I complemented these readings with a book from the library entitled Liberating Visions: Human Fulfillment and Social Justice in African American Thought by Robert Franklin. I also purchased a book entitled <u>Ethics for the New Millennium</u> by the Dalai Lama.

These writings were overwhelmingly male- or euro-centric, but they were the beginnings of the answers to my questions on finding purpose and fulfillment. In later years, I would be exposed to a wider spectrum of authors including: Bell Hooks, Nikki Giovanni, Alice Walker, Zora Neale Hurston, Maya Angelou, and others.

The following are excerpts from these influential authors in no particular order. Each of these philosophers pointed me to a greater understanding of life and a multi-dimensional approach to my existence and a better understanding of my mental health.

Historical Views on the Three Dimensions of Life

Booker T. Washington[9]

"The perfect man is to come through a systematic and harmonious development of mind, body, and soul (Harlan, 1972 p. 5)," Washington writes of a holistic view of individual development. The moral person evolves towards maturity only insofar as he or she is challenged systematically to develop physically, intellectually, and spiritually. Education is the means by which such development is achieved. The end of this

---

[9] Picture from https://www.blackfacts.com/fact/booker-t-washington-biography

process should manifest itself as a productive hardworking person who contributes to the "wealth, happiness, and permanent prosperity of the society." He emphasized the ability and obligation of every person to become an economically resourceful, self-determining agent (Franklin, 1990 p. 18)."

W.E.B. Du Bois[10]

"Life is the fullest, most complete enjoyment of the

 possibilities of human existence. It is the development and broadening of the feelings and emotions through sound and color, line and form. Its technical mastery of the media that these paths and emotions need for expression of their full meaning. It is the free enjoyment of every normal appetite. It is giving reign to the creative impulse, in thought and imagination. Here roots rise of the joy of living, of music, painting, drawing, sculpture and building, hence rise literature with romance, poetry and essay, hence rise love, friendship, emulation, and ambition, and ever widening realms of thought in increasing circles of apprehended and interpreted truth (From *Du Bois Speaks* 1890-19910 p.11)."

Du Bois saw education as a pathway to higher living. Du Bois writes, "[education provides] a glimpse of the higher life, the broader possibilities of humanity, which is granted to the man who, amid the rush of living, pauses for short years to learn what living means (Franklin, 1990 p.61)."

---

[10] Picture from https://www.biography.com/activist/web-du-bois

DuBois saw faith as an open complaint to God. "Why did God make me an outcast and stranger in my own house (DuBois 1903, p.221)." DuBois spoke about a world which gives a Black man no true self-consciousness. DuBois argued that formal freedom from slavery had brought no "real" freedom, in that most African Americans still live in the shadows of slavery, utter poverty, broken homes, war, racism, and capitalism. Dubois argued "to be a poor man is hard, but to be a poor race in the land of the dollar is the very bottom of hardships (p. 219)."

Dr. Martin Luther King, Jr.[11]
In Martin Luther King's writing "The Dimensions of a Complete Life" from "The Measure of a Man," King writes,

"There are three dimensions of a complete life: length,

breadth, and height. The length of life is not its duration or its longevity, but it is the push of life forward to achieve its personal ends and ambitions. It is the inward concern for one's own welfare. The individual is concerned with developing his inner powers. It is that dimension of life in which the individual pursues personal ends and ambitions. The breath of life is that dimension of life in which we are concerned about others. An individual has not started living until he (or she) can rise above the narrow confines

---

[11] Picture from https://www.huffpost.com/entry/remembering-martin-luther-king-jr_b_6471172

of his (or her) individualistic concerns to the broader concerns of all humanity. Finally, there is a third dimension. Some people never get beyond the first two dimensions of life, they develop their inner powers, they love humanity, but they stop right here. If we are to live a complete life we must reach up and discover God (King, 1959 p.29)."

Aristotle[12]

In Aristotle's <u>On Happiness,</u> he writes about the multiple dimensions of the human experience. First, he discusses

the 'virtue' of the work we perform through our bodies (i.e. carpenter or harpist). Secondly, he discusses the 'rationale element' as the mind, and thirdly the "activity of the soul."

Aristotle writes, "Is it then possible that while the carpenter and a shoemaker have their own proper functions and spheres of action, man as man (or woman as woman) has none, but was left by nature a good-for-nothing without a function? Should we not assume that just as the eye, the hand, the foot and in general each part of the body clearly has its own proper function, so man (or woman) too has some function over and above the functions of his (or her) parts? What can this function possibly be, simply living?" He shares that even with plants, there remains then an active life of the 'rational element' (The Great Books Foundation 1990, p7).

---

[12] Picture from https://www.thefamouspeople.com/profiles/aristotle-116.php

The proper function of man, then, consists of an activity of the soul in conformity with a rational principle or at least not without it. In speaking of the proper function of a given individual, we mean that it is the same in kind as the function of an individual who sets higher standards for himself (or herself): the proper function for a harpist for example, is the same as a harpist who has set high standards for himself (or herself). The same applies to every group of individuals: the full attainment of excellence must be added to the mere function. In other words, the function of the harpist is to play the harp; the function of the harpist who has high standards is to play it well. On these assumptions, if we take the proper function of man to be a certain kind of life, and if this kind of life is an <u>activity of the soul.</u> Then actions performed in conjunction with the <u>rational element (mind)</u>, of high standards is he (or she) who performs these actions well and properly. If a function is well performed in accordance with the excellence appropriate to it; we reach the conclusion that the good of man is an <u>activity of the soul</u> in conformity with <u>excellence or virtue</u> (The Great Books Foundation 1990, p8).

John Dewey[13]

In John Dewey's <u>Habits and Will,</u> he discusses body, mind, and character. He writes,

"They suppose that if one is told what to do, if the *right* end is pointed to them, all that is required in order to bring about the right act is will or wish on the part of the one who is to act. An illustration, the matter of physical posture; the assumption is that if a man (or woman) is told to stand up straight all that is further needed is wish and effort on his part and the deed is done the prevalence of this belief, starting with false notions about control of the <u>body</u> and extending to control of <u>mind</u> and <u>character</u> is the greatest bar to intelligent social progress (The Great Books Foundation 1990, p.19)."

Dewey describes how purposeful people get to a desired end by accomplishing small victories along the route. Dewey writes,

"The "end" is merely a series of acts viewed at a remote stage and the means is merely the series viewed at an earlier one. The distinction of means and end arises surveying the *course* of a proposed *line* of action, a connected series in time. The "end" is the last act thought of; the means are the acts to

---

[13] Picture from https://www.amazon.com/John-Dewey-150-Reflections-Century/dp/1557535507

be performed prior to it in time. To *reach* an end we must take our minds off from it and attend to the act which is next to be performed prior to it in time. We must make that the end (The Great Books Foundation 1990, p.23)."

Immanuel Kant[14]

The philosopher, Immanuel Kant, spoke of purpose and humanity through the lens of our internal debate between good and evil or selfishness versus selflessness.

Kant writes,

"Man (or woman) and generally any rational being exist as an end in himself (or herself) not merely as a means to be arbitrarily used by this or that will, but in all his (or her) actions, whether they concern himself or other rational beings, must be regarded at the same time as an end. [Enlightenment] is man's emergence from his self-imposed nonage. Nonage is the inability to use one's own understanding without another's guidance. This nonage is self-imposed if its cause lies not in lack of understanding but in indecision and lack of courage to use one's own mind without another's guidance. <u>Dare to know</u>. (The Great Books Foundation 1990, p.90)"

---

[14] Picture from https://cla.umn.edu/philosophy/news-events/story/kant-polymath-modern-thought

Kant described conscience as an internal prosecutor that helps us to align our actions with purpose and humanity. Kant writes,

> "We find in our hearts a prosecutor for who there would be no place, unless there was also a law. This law, which is based on reason and not sentiment is incorruptible and incontestably just and pure it is the moral law, established as the holy and inviolable law of humanity (The Great Books Foundation 1990, p.96)."

Dalai Lama[15]

In the book Ethics for the New Millennium, the Dalai Lama discusses the myth of money versus purpose. He writes,

"Everywhere by all means imaginable people are striving to improve their lives. Yet strangely my impression is those living in the materially developed countries with all their industry are in some ways less satisfied, are less happy, and to some extent suffer more than those who live in the least developed countries... They are so caught up in the idea of requiring still more that they make no room for anything else in their lives. In their absorption, they actually lose the dream of happiness, which riches were to have provided. As

---

[15] Picture from https://www.quotemirror.com/quote-1417448880/

a result, they are constantly tormented torn between doubt and what might happen and the hope of gaining more and plagued with mental and emotional suffering (Lama 2001, p.5)."

The Dalai Lama sees the multiple dimensions of the human experience on three levels. He writes,

"We can understand how things and events come to be [16]in three different ways. At the first level, the principle of cause and effect where all things and events arise in <u>dependence on a complex web of inter-related causes and conditions</u>...the second level can be understood in terms of <u>mutual dependence</u> which exists between parts and a whole. The idea of 'whole' is predicated on parts, but these parts themselves must be considered to be wholes comprised of their own parts.... On the third level, all phenomena can be understood to be <u>dependently originated</u>, because when we analyze them, we find that, ultimately, they lack independent identity. For example, let's take the relationship between parent or child. Someone is a parent only because he or she has children. Likewise, a daughter or son is so called only in relation to them having parents (Lama 2001, p.37)."

---

[16] Picture from https://thediplomat.com/2014/09/the-dalai-lama-and-the-politics-of-reincarnation/

The Multiple Dimensions of the Human Experience

As we briefly looked at the work of. Booker T. Washington, W.E.B. DuBois, Dr. Martin Luther King Jr, Aristotle, John Dewey, Immanuel Kant, and the Dalai Lama, they all point to the multi-dimensional nature of the human experience. Each sees life differently, but all conclude that there is more to life than what the eyes can see. They all conclude that there are elements of human existence that stretch past one dimension. In the following table, I perform a meta-analysis of the multi-dimensional approaches of each author.

Table: Historical Thought on the 3 Dimensions of Life

Author	Dimension 1	Dimension 2	Dimension 3
Dr. Martin Luther King Jr.	**Length**- Material Ambition	**Breath**- Concern for Humanity	**Depth**- Discover God
W.E.B. DuBois	**Human Existence**- broadening of feeling and emotion	**Education**- Higher living	**Question**-Why did God make me an outcast and stranger in my own house?
Booker T. Washington	**Body**- Hard work contributes to society (business ownership, trades, and agriculture)	**Mind**- Education is the solution	**Soul**- Self-determining agent
Aristotle	**Activity**- Proper function (i.e. harpist, shoemaker, carpenter)	**Mind**- The rational element	**Soul**- Excellence and Virtue
John Dewey	**Body**- Physical control	**Mind**- Wish and effort	**Character**- Greatest measure of intelligent social progress
Immanuel Kant	**Body**- The place which holds our rational mind and conscience	**Mind**- To be enlightened is to understand without another's guidance	**Conscience**- Moral and Holy law of humanity
Dalai Lama	**Cause and Effect**- Dependence on a complex web of inter-related causes and conditions	**Mutual Dependence**- Exists between parts and a whole	**Dependently Originated**- Lack independent identity

As noted in the table, these philosophers look at lifestyle as a process that involves multiple dimensions of the human experience. The goal of the 31 Kings Mental Health Game is to balance physical health and spiritual health with the renewing of a purposeful mind. Therefore, it is not beneficial to continue to look at the concepts of mental health through a one-dimensional lens, but rather to begin being more aware of the multiple layers involved in producing a mentally healthy lifestyle. We should not be ruled by the impulses of our body or the fleeting thoughts of our mind. The delicate balance of body, mind, and spirit requires a discipline that is conscious and aware of each of the dimensions of self and how they impact one another. Each lifestyle is different just as different body types are needed for different types of work, and varying levels of mental aptitude are required for varying types of work. Instead of prescribing a specific solution for all of humanity, I work to become more conscious and aware of my own physical, mental, and spiritual health in preparation for my purposeful work. Likewise, it is the assignment for us all to spend time feeding the body, mind, and spirit to improve overall wellbeing and mental health.

The Body

"The most important of our physical creation for all of us is our own body. The physical body is the first gift for that which we are aware of. It is the ultimate machine. (Sadhguru, 2016 p.89)"

Having a healthy body is directly related to a healthy mind. My family has a history of high blood pressure and hypertension. If I believe in improving the human condition, then I must be serious about my physical and mental health. I must be conscious about what I eat along with my caloric intake, exercise, meditation, and sleep. It does me no good if I become the best professor if I can't make it to class because I'm sick all the time or can't make it up the stairs without pausing to catch my breath. What is the point if I can give an elegant speech or write a great book, if I can no longer bend down to clip my toenails because my gut has impeded my bend and my hamstrings are tighter than the strings of a guitar?

Our body is the physical manifestation of our purpose on the earth. This wondrous vessel in which we interact with the earth, the sea, the sand, oh and yes other people. The body is what we use to express touch when we shake a hand, to greet another person with a hug, or to glare with the eyes.

Nutrition
In the book Dr. Wright's Guide to Healing with Nutrition by Jonathan Wrights, M.D., the author uses the following story to drive home the point that our bodies weren't made to eat the; canned goods, high sugar, and high preservative He writes,

The four women had wandered far to find food for the mid-day meal. Finally, the oldest, wise in the ways of their tribe, saw a familiar plant. She'd seen it only once as a girl, but had remembered it. From it, they gathered <u>cans of spaghetti</u> and meatballs, and started home.(p.5)

The point Dr. Wright is driving home is, 'we can't find <u>cans of spaghetti</u> in nature'. They are products of industry and industry is killing our physical health. In recent history, "agriculture and large-scale domestication of cows, pigs, chickens, and other food animals is relatively in its infancy in the whole history of man (p.5)." It is important that each of us examine our diet and nutritional intake with a nutritionist and/or naturopathic doctor. It is not the goal here to provide every nutritional solution, but to make the reader aware (or re-aware) of the importance of nutrition to health and our purposeful work. Every cell in the body is connected and works together to produce optimal physical and mental health. Dr. Wright explains, "no part of our bodies can stay as healthy as possible without the flow of nutrients for growth and repair (p.563)." Along with a proper diet for energy and nutritional supplements, our bodies need regular exercise to prevent mental stress, illness, and injury.

The Gut

There is increasing evidence on the connections between gut health and mental health[17] [18]. In the National Institute of Health study entitled <u>The Gut-Brain Axis: The Missing Link in Depression</u>[19], the research concluded,

> Based on evidence, the gut microbiota is associated with metabolic disorders such as obesity, diabetes mellitus and neuropsychiatric disorders such as schizophrenia, autistic disorders, anxiety disorders and major depressive disorders. In the past few years, neuroscientific research has shown the importance of the microbiota in the development of brain systems.

I get the gut is important but for the majority of my life I have not been intentionally caring for my gut. My question was, what is a practical way I can improve my gut health through a daily lifestyle change? My answer came from a surprising source. I had heard a few times about the gut benefits of Apple Cider Vinegar with the Mother (good bacteria), but whenever I tried it, it tasted so strong and bad it turned me off from taking it.

---

[17] Dash, S., Clarke, G., Berk, M., & Jacka, F. N. (2015). The gut microbiome and diet in psychiatry: focus on depression. *Current opinion in psychiatry, 28*(1), 1-6.

[18] Peirce, J. M., & Alviña, K. (2019). The role of inflammation and the gut microbiome in depression and anxiety. *Journal of neuroscience research, 97*(10), 1223-1241.

[19] Evrensel, A., & Ceylan, M. E. (2015). The gut-brain axis: the missing link in depression. *Clinical Psychopharmacology and Neuroscience, 13*(3), 239.

Then this past fall I was traveling on an unexpected trip to Charlotte, North Carolina to care for my father who recently had a hip operation. I was driving a lot, staying in hotels, and eating a lot of fast food. All of these lifestyle activities were terrible for my gut health and I could feel it. I was sluggish, tired, and bloated. The reminder of the solution came from a surprising source. When I was checking in late to a hotel the desk clerk and I were having a casual conversation and small talk when he went off on a tangent and said 'My number two's used to be so bad almost every time I went, it was mostly watery, then my wife told me to mix a teaspoon of apple cider vinegar and drink it in a cup of water, since then my number two's have been great. It's amazing that just a little a day keeps my system well. I try more every so often and it doesn't work as well as a little teaspoon daily."

This desk clerk's random advice finally hit home as my gut was battling my poor lifestyle choices. In reflection, I don't know if that desk clerk was an angel or was sent to give me that message at that time. But it changed my gut health for the rest of my life. I began drinking a teaspoon of apple cider vinegar with good bacteria daily with water, and my gut and mind have been better ever since. Now when I taste apple cider vinegar with water, it actually tastes good, because my brain tells my taste buds, we need this in our body. Another alternative is taking probiotics.

Exercise
In graduate school at the University of North Carolina, I lived a sedentary lifestyle and sat all day reading, in traffic, writing etc.. Because of all my graduate school sitting, my

health began to decline. I decided to participate in a study at UNC-Chapel Hill led by Dr. Candice Alick. The study was life changing and transformative. It was not that I did not know how important exercise and diet monitoring was to my mental and physical health. I just did not know how to do it as a middle-aged adult. When I was younger, activity was a natural part of my life, but as I've grown older the nature of my work has become largely sedentary. I would wake up, sit for breakfast, sit and make a few calls, then sit in my car for my commute and then come to class, sit and take notes, or sit and type a paper or article. I think you get the point.

I do a lot of sitting and exercise was not a part of my regular regiment before participating in this weight loss study. If anything, the study made me more conscious and aware of my lack of activity and high caloric diet. During the study, I used a mobile app to help me keep track of health statistics. For the first two weeks of the study, Dr. Alick made me track every meal, every sip of water, every beer, and all exercise and activity. As I began to look at how many calories I was consuming versus how many calories I was burning, it was no wonder my health was declining. I was on the way to the grave and being escorted by Krispy Kreme doughnuts. In the article Sitting is the New Smoking, the authors note most Americans sit 10 hours per day. The article states,

> Research suggests that sedentary lifestyles are themselves a risk factor for cardiometabolic morbidity (Baddeley, 2016 p.258).

I challenge you to do the same thing Dr. Alick challenged me to do. For two weeks track your diet down to every single thing you eat or drink and track your daily fitness activity using a mobile app. There are a plethora of mobile apps that can easily calculate every meal or food item you consume along with the calories you can burn daily from a variety of exercise activities. Below you can see a screenshot of my recent daily step activity. My goal is to do 10,000 steps per day. Sometimes I hit my goal and sometimes I don't. But I have found being more conscious of my daily step count helps to keep me become more accountable to myself for my level of physical activity.

Derrick's Weekly Step Tracking

As you can see, I don't always hit my goal, but simply having a goal helps me to be conscious about my physical activity. By no means am I an expert, but I did lose 20 pounds during the weight loss study and have managed to keep it off. However, my confession is I still have a cup of coffee and a doughnut next to me right now as I type. The only difference between me now and me before the study, is that I changed my lens on health. Now, I hit the treadmill for 20 minutes before or after I eat the same donut. I don't have it figured out, but I know it's important to be more conscious of everything I eat and stay active daily. Even if you don't have it figured out, it's ok. By being conscious, it can help you move closer to the model of health you desire to perform your purpose with endurance and patience.

Rest
Equally as important to the body as diet and exercise is rest. Rest is the restorative physical action that improves brain function and mental health. Yet, rest is also often a conscious choice. We have to make a conscious decision to increase or decrease the amount of sleep we are getting daily for optimal mental health. Like my physical activity, I have often overlooked 8 hours of sleep a day as being essential to my mental health. In college I learned, by burning the midnight oil, writing papers was the model of a "good" student. Now I realize proper rest, a good diet, and exercise make writing light and easy, instead of an all night wrestling match with my typing.

It is recommended to sleep 6 to 8 hours per day to initiate the restorative physical and mental healing processes. I have found when I don't get proper rest, I'm not the best teacher or researcher. The ways in which I have operated my grant writing business have often prevented me from getting proper rest. There have been too many nights where I've been working until the late hours staring at a blue screen and typing. I know this is not good for me. As I've gotten older, I now realize that even a quick power nap will improve my productivity. Many smart watches and mobile apps can now track your sleep. By tracking my sleep similarly to tracking my diet and exercise, it helped me to become more conscious of my decision-making power on when to go to sleep and why.

I challenge you to download an app or get an inexpensive wrist monitor to measure your sleep for two weeks and increase your consciousness of your sleeping quota. You can use many apps to measure the amount, quality, and/or stages of your sleep. My wife bought me a fitness watch[20] to monitor my health and I tracked one week of my sleep (depicted below). The activity was revealing and helped me to begin to create lifestyle strategies to get better sleep, like keeping a more disciplined sleep schedule and meditating for five minutes before I go to sleep.

[20] Smartwatches emit small amounts of radiation, use in moderation.

Derrick's Fitness Watch Sleep Study

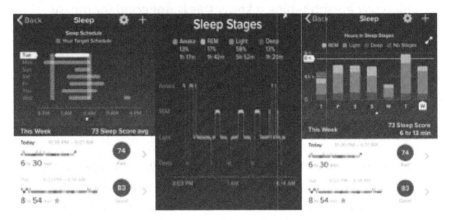

Improving my sleep helped my mental health and my life. By tracking and improving the quality of my sleep, it helps me to slightly adjust my habits (i.e. going to bed earlier) and to move towards a more purposeful and abundant lifestyle. A lifestyle with exercise, proper rest, prayer, and meditation makes stress dissipate like mist in the air. If we choose not to accept and receive stress, it will not impact our mental and/or physical health. Even though stressors are real in our lives, when we *choose* not to absorb the stress, it is as if stress itself doesn't exist in our realities.

Stress Doesn't Exist

Why does the same stressful event impact two different people in vastly different ways? For one person going through a stressful event, their heart rate increases, mental health declines, and their spirit fades. For another person going through the exact same stressful event, they can react with calm, peace, and even become more inspirational. It is because stress doesn't exist. Stress is really a concept that describes how we react to the daily hurdles, challenges, and traumas of life. Like any other concept, our mental lens can determine stresses' power over our lives, our coping strategies, and resilience. In addition, when we prepare our bodies through nutrition, exercise, and rest, it helps us to overcome the daily stressors in life instead of succumbing to them. We can also prepare our minds by nurturing, exercising, and resting our brains.

In the book, The Relaxation Response by Herbert Benson, M.D., he highlights research on the causation of hypertension, strokes, and heart attacks, then points to meditation as the solution. Dr. Benson writes,

> Decreases of the heart and brain account for 50% of the deaths in the United States...various degrees of hypertension are present in 15 to 33 percent of the U.S. population...we are not generally aware that the disease is slowly developing within us (p.19)

Dr. Benson goes on to describe the causes of hypertension. He writes,
> The traditional explanations have been 1) inappropriate diet, 2) lack of exercise, and 3) family disposition. Yet there is another factor which has often been ignored: environmental stress. (p.20)

Meditation

Dr. Benson then points to meditation as a solution to eliminating the harmful effects of environmental stress. He prescribes the following method as a solution,

> You will find that evoking the relaxation response is extremely simple if you follow a very short set of instructions which incorporate four essential elements:
>
> 1) a quiet environment;
> 2) a mental device such as a word or phrase which should be repeated in a specific fashion over and over again;
> 3) the adoption of a passive (trusting) attitude, which is perhaps the most important of the elements and
> 4) a comfortable position. Your appropriate practice of these four elements for ten to twenty minutes once or twice daily should markedly enhance your well-being.(p.21)

You can make any changes to this process that fit your mind, body, and spirit. A friend, and business coach, Barron Damon, leads meditation by repeating the word "Release." For faith-based groups, he uses the word "Jesus". I use both and other words that relate to the needs of my meditation practice for that specific day. I also combine meditation with Yoga and Tai Chi, which both provide additional physical and exercise benefits. I have found that meditating, or practicing Yoga or Tai Chi, while being immersed in nature and understanding our connection with nature is extremely effective and can help improve blood pressure, mental health, and general quality of life.

Nature

Like meditation, nature has mentally healing qualities that help me to reconnect and re-center. Research is now finding nature, outdoors, and exposure to sunlight improve mental health[21]. I've always been attracted to the water i.e. lakes, beaches, and ponds, but I haven't known just how therapeutic nature was until recently. About 9 months into my NSF grant research, I was at home grilling. The weather began to lightly drizzle. I brushed it off and continued to grill in the rain. Then, lightning began to strike, but I felt 'I was already committed to these burgers so let me just finish right quick before the lightning gets any worse'. This was a stupid decision.

As I stood outside, a crack of lightning hit my home and it felt like the ground and everything I was attached to was rocked violently. My body was thrown against my back door and I hit headfirst. In retrospect, I don't actually know if I was hit by lightning or if the sheer sound of the lightning when it hit my house frightened me so much I jumped back into the house. Since I don't fully remember the exact events, it depends on the audience if I tell the story like a hero or a coward. Either way, I should not have been grilling out in a lightning storm. The lightning blew

---

[21] Sciulli, N., Goullet, D., & Snell, T. (2022). Working from Home with a View of Nature (and Sunlight) Benefits People's Well-Being. *Ecopsychology.*

out my air conditioning unit and blew some fuses in the house but thank God, I was alive.

This was the first time in my life I had a brain injury. Recovering from the concussion was difficult. When I initially met with a neurologist, I was having 5 to 6 headaches per day. I couldn't look at a computer or cell phone without a splitting pain in my head. I was scared. I had been making my living by using my brain for most of my life and here it was not working at its full capacity. My workdays were cut from 8 to10 hours of intense thinking to about 30 minutes a day. There was nothing I could do to speed up this recovery. It was frustrating and I'm sure I was short tempered with my wife and my staff. After cutting off the TV and cell phone, I tried to figure out a way not to think too deeply or too much, so I began gardening. There was something about the manipulation of dirt, watering the plants, and working to keep something alive that in turn healed me. Helping to keep the smallest seeds of God's creation alive gave me purpose and gave me healing.

In the book The Will to Meaning by psychotherapist Viktor Frankl, the author makes the connection between having a clear purpose and its relationship to physical and mental health. Frankl writes,

> A strong meaning orientation is a health-promoting and life-prolonging, if not life preserving, agent. It not only makes for physical but also for mental health (Frankl, 2014 p.48).

After being cleared by my neurologist I reflected and realized the concussion, though painful, was a good thing because it helped me to learn <u>I needed to slow down and appreciate life, my loved ones, purpose, and nature</u>. I found a connection with trees, birds, and deer that I had not noticed before. There was nature teeming all around me every day, but in the midst of my research, my work schedule, and rushing in traffic to run errands, get groceries, and pick up my daughter from afterschool I ignored the beauty of nature that I was immersed in every day.

Dirt and Gardening

Putting my hands in the dirt and soil while gardening was healing for me. It helped me to go back to the earth and reconnect with how the earth keeps all of its creatures and plants alive. A naturopathic doctor, Patricia Crisp, told me to sit barefoot in grass for about 20 minutes to reconnect with the earth. I know it sounds weird, but it worked. If it even had a placebo effect on me, it changed my condition, my perspective, and made my life more intentional. If you haven't done this before, sit barefoot on the ground and see how you feel. For me, looking at the flowers in my garden helped my mind to focus on the beauty of nature and calm my mental state.

The Mind and Emotions

'The mind is fickle and flighty, it flies after fancies
wherever it likes: it is difficult indeed to restrain. But it is
a great good to control the mind; a mind self-controlled is
a source of great joy'
(Dhammapada, verse 35).

The mind can be like a mental soundtrack we carry with us
all day. It's like that song, tune, or commercial we can't get
out of our heads. Sometimes it's a good song and
sometimes it's that annoying commercial jingle. For many
of us, we are a passenger, and the mind takes us wherever
it wants to go from thoughts of happiness to thoughts of
depression. Similarly, our emotions are tied to our
thoughts and can take us for a trip from deep feelings of
pain and despair to an inner peace rooted in hope,
purpose, and destiny.

There are a number of methods and resources that can
help us take back control of our thoughts and emotions.
For me, since my identity is reflected through my faith,
scripture is an effective tool for reminding me who I am
and getting my mind back on the right track. Additional
tools I use are meditation, yoga, poetry, songwriting, and
conversations with friends, family, or a professional
therapist. I have found when conversing with other
people, I need to be sure they are speaking life into my
thoughts and not doubt and fear. These people should be
vetted by your past interactions. Even those we love can
have a bad day and speak words to you that begin to make
you question your purpose and identity.

I had one of these experiences when I was teaching undergrad students at the University of North Carolina at Chapel Hill. I was on my way to work and in the car with a friend. As we were driving to the campus, we got into one of those car arguments. You know the ones that are really for no reason at all except you are both stuck in a small metal box together and neither one of you can jump out of the moving car. It was bad. As I finally got out of the car and was walking to my class to ironically teach on finding purpose, my spirit was down, and my mind was stuck in a mode where I was developing mental responses to the previous argument instead of mentally preparing myself for my students. I tried to think of something else, but my mind and emotions were stuck in a funk. I had five minutes before class, and at this rate, I was not going to be able to give my students my best mind and emotions. When this happens to teachers, it is easy to go to the classroom and go through the motions. Some teachers don't see every split second as a chance to transform the lives of our students and ourselves.

I went to my phone, opened the Bible app and looked for a scripture. My spirit began to tell me what scripture I needed to remind myself of. It was something about *'wonderfully created'* but I could not remember it. So, I typed in wonderfully created in the search box and the scripture I needed to reset my mind and emotions appeared in the results.

> *"I will praise thee; for I am fearfully and wonderfully made: marvelous are thy works; and that my soul knoweth well."*

After reading this three-times, it began to replay itself in my mind and my emotions and spirit began to digest the meaning. Instantly, the thoughts of self-doubt, guilt, and anxiety left me, and I began to thank God for making me through a delicately fearful and wonderful process. I also thanked God for reminding me each one of my students were marvelous, like the beauty of the ocean or the calm of the morning. This meant I needed to get out of my funk and treat my students with the understanding that they were wonderfully made. Everything from the way I stood, to my walk, to my gate began to change and wrap itself around this scripture. As I walked into the classroom, I carried this energy of intentionality with me and smiled at my students as if God had spit them out of the womb that morning. By using the tool of scripture, I was able to take back control of my mind and emotions.

You have this same power, and it can be done in a plethora of ways. It doesn't have to be the scripture I used. You can find a statement, positive mantra, or affirmation that works for you and do that. The key is to set your mind and take control of wavering thoughts that can be detrimental to your purpose driven work.

Gratitude
There is increasing empirical evidence that being grateful and expressing gratitude improves mental health[22]. This science can be seen in many faith traditions and has proven to be effective. Keeping the mind in a state of gratefulness prevents the mind from perseverating on

---

[22] Petrocchi, N., & Couyoumdjian, A. (2016). The impact of gratitude on depression and anxiety: the mediating role of criticizing, attacking, and reassuring the self. *Self and Identity*, *15*(2), 191-205.

complaints, self-critiques, and operating in a victim mindset. A victim mindset is crippling because it gives me no hope of improvement, it tells me there is nothing I can do to change my life situation, because I'm a victim. Shifting my mind towards gratitude also helps me from keeping my mind away from dwelling on negative memories from my past, my regrets, and shame. The activity that has been the most helpful for me in shifting my mind towards gratitude is our nightly 'family thankful' prayers. It takes maybe 3 minutes, but my wife, my daughter and I share what we are grateful for that day. Whether these things are seemingly small like spending time with a friend or arriving home safely from a trip, they help my mind shift before I go to sleep. Another effective daily lifestyle activity is to keep a gratitude journal, listing what you are grateful for.

Formerly Isolated

Research now finds that isolation causes depression and anxiety[23], and we have all experienced isolation. The term formerly isolated refers to all Americans in the post 2020 quarantine isolation era. These Americans all experienced a slow-down in their daily activities due to mandatory and voluntary quarantines and isolations. It is important to value relationships with family, friends, co-workers and your chosen faith/ affinity community. As we get older, we can tend to have less friends. That is when it's even more important to schedule interactions with friends. Even if it

---

[23] Han, R. T., Kim, Y. B., Park, E. H., Kim, J. Y., Ryu, C., Kim, H. Y., ... & Na, H. S. (2018). Long-term isolation elicits depression and anxiety-related behaviors by reducing oxytocin-induced GABAergic transmission in central amygdala. *Frontiers in molecular neuroscience*, *11*, 246.

is a long-awaited trip to go see an old friend, plan it today because tomorrow is not promised.

This population also received the benefits of experiencing life at a slower pace and many have decided to continue to work from home and a variety of other health and life choices as a result of being "Formerly Isolated".

Silence

Similar to meditation, practicing silence can have positive health effects. I used to be one of those professors who just liked to hear themselves talk. I would talk all the time, even when it was not necessary. This prevented me from using a dialogical teaching style, because I would fill all the silence with my voice. Research finds that if teachers ask a question to their class or an individual student that they should wait at least 10 seconds to allow the student(s) to process the question and reply. For me, I would give about 5 seconds, then answer myself and move onto the next topic. When I did this, the classroom became an arena for my ego instead of a place where any real learning, contemplation, and growth could occur. If you teach the way I did, please stop it. Be silent and listen.

Steven Covey discusses this in his book, the 7 Habits of Highly effective People. He writes the key to communication is to "listen first and speak second." This requires silence and a comfortability with silence that gives the other person psychological air and space to communicate. This concept is also found in ancient spiritual text.

> "Let every man be swift to hear, slow to speak, and slow to wrath." (James 1:9)

This quality of being silent also positions me as a listener and learner. It's important that we don't believe we have arrived and know it all. It's important to adopt the paradigm of a lifelong learner.

A Learner's Lens[24]
When we look at life through a learner's lens, we look for lessons in the breeze of the wind and the glimmer of sunlight in the morning. More importantly, we don't turn off our learning brain. Some people after they earn degrees and accolades, switch off the learning part of their brain and only use the teaching parts of their brain. A technique that I've learned overtime which helps me is to position my body as a learner.

When someone else is speaking to me, I make eye contact with them, lean a little bit towards the speaker and even gently mirror their body language (this helps the speaker to subconsciously feel comfortable with you.) Now I am ready to learn.

---

[24] Picture from MS Word 2020 Clipart

Spirit

"If God had'na given me a song to sing, I wouldn't have a song to sing. The song comes from God, all the time"
- Bob Marley (Worth, 1995 p. 31)

As noted in the section on the three dimensions of the human experience, we have a physical body, mind/emotions, and a spirit[25]. However, the part of us we often overlook and wouldn't be covered in a training book is our spirit. The spirit may be the most essential part of ourselves that we need when helping others to navigate through their purpose. In the book <u>Applying Islamic Principles to Clinical Mental Health Care: Introducing Traditional Islamically Integrated Psychotherapy,</u> the authors find a connection between spiritual health and mental health. The research team of Islamic psychotherapist authors used the term psycho-spiritual health to articulate this intimate connection between mind and spirit. They write,

> *maintenance of psycho-spiritual health is critical to human functioning in Islam more important in fact than the sustenance of the physical body[26]*

---

[25] The goal of my work is not for the reader to adopt my exact spiritual views but rather, ask the question, what impact does my spirit have on my mental health? For readers who see the world through an agnostic and/or atheist lens this part of the book and game can be a tool to track and encourage all 'other' elements that impact your mental health outside of Body and Mind. These may include affinity groups or supportive people with values and reinforcing perspectives.

[26] Keshavarzi, H., Khan, F., Ali, B., & Awaad, R. (Eds.). (2020). *Applying Islamic principles to clinical mental health care: Introducing traditional Islamically integrated psychotherapy.* Routledge.

These psychotherapists discuss Tradition Islamic Integrated Psychotherapy (TIIP) as a holistic approach to the construction of a spiritually integrated psychology. Through TIIP, therapists are finding increasingly improving results when Islamic patients are given mental health treatment that incorporates their spiritual practice and belief system. Their work not only points to the connection of spirituality and mental health, but also suggests spiritual health may be a more determining factor in mental health than physical health and inflammation in the body.

The spirit is the part of the three dimensions of self that is the hardest to explain, to test empirically, or to understand how to feed and nurture. Some call this part of ourselves the soul, personality, or energetic force.

Soul
Many faith traditions describe this third spiritual part of ourselves as the soul. In addition to being my favorite type of food (lol), our soul is the unseen part of us that we communicate to everyone. In identity research, this part of our uniqueness is often manifested and explained as personality. It is what makes you "you."

Personality
Your personality is your unique swagger. It's what attracts people to you or repels people from you. It's what makes you different and when honed, it can be the key to your success. People want to do business with people they know, trust, and like. Even if your client knows you are the best in the world and builds trust in you due to your history of work and references, if you are a jerk, you will

not keep the client. Being likable is not easy, but it's real. It's that unspoken thing about you that can help you in times of need. Your personality revolves around you like a spiritual energy force and transforms your environments. When you walk on purpose, your energy bends reality around you in the direction of your purpose.

Energy
Sadruguru writes,

> 'Your memory and your imagination which includes your ideas, beliefs, and emotions-belong to the psychological realm [the mind]. Life can be tasted and transcended only when there is a distinction between the psychological [the mind] and the existential [the energetic or spiritual] (p.211).'

You have a spiritual energy in you and around you that impacts your mental state. Energy can be seen as positive/ high vibration energy or a negative/low vibration energy or somewhere on the continuum in between. The energy we carry can be helped by how we treat our body, mind, emotions, and spirit. When all of these are flowing well, our energy is contagious. It becomes the secret ingredient to getting things done while living mentally at peace. In the Hindu[27] tradition, it is the primordial cosmic energy, female in aspect, and represents the dynamic forces that are thought to move through the universe.

My goal here is not to advocate for any specific spiritual practice as the fit for all. The main point I want the reader

---

[27] Feuerstein, Georg (2000). *The Shambhala Encyclopedia of Yoga.* Boston, MA: Shambhala Publications.

to think deeply about is that there is some spiritual or energetic element to our existence and this element can greatly impact our mental health if we are not spiritually healthy. I work towards spiritual health by doing activities that feed my spiritual self.

Feeding the Spirit Daily

Through the physical health study with Dr. Alick, I began to become more conscious of what I ate every day and the calories I burned through exercise. My unhealthy overweight lifestyle was due to my daily lifestyle and mindless eating and lack of exercise. I didn't gain all my weight in one day or at one big Thanksgiving meal, it was a result of a daily lifestyle of poor health choices. I learned that in order to begin my physical health journey, I needed to adopt a daily plan and work the plan day by day. After day one of eating well and exercising, I looked at the scale and nothing happened. Somehow I had to adopt the belief that these small daily changes would eventually manifest in improved physical health. They did. After 90 days of this new active lifestyle, I had lost 20lbs and was feeling physically better. Similarly, my mental health recovery was not an overnight miracle but a product of daily meditation, gardening, silence, gratitude journaling, sleep, etc.. Gradually, I began to see improvement in my temperament, joy, and mental control over fleeting defeating thoughts. Instead of dwelling on negative mental thoughts, the practice of meditation and mindfulness gave me a greater understanding of the power I have to control what I think about and what thoughts I let go.

If we understand that our physical bodies need a healthy diet, good gut bacteria, and regular exercise to produce a healthy body. Then we also understand how we must daily feed our 'Spirit' through lifestyle choices. The major lifestyle change that helped my spiritual growth was reading the Bible daily and listening to a short sermon or spiritual message. I downloaded a Bible reading mobile app and joined a "Bible in a Year" reading plan. Each day, I would read and/or listen to 10-15 minutes of the Bible and combine it with prayer and study. After day one of this spiritual practice, just like the physical exercise, I saw no change. But over time in small ways, I began to draw closer to God and feel God's presence in my life and decision making. I was even able to see new revelations for my life through scripture. This happened one day while I was brushing my teeth and listening to the Bible app.

The mobile app was reading aloud the scripture Joshua 12:7-24. It reads

> *7 Here is a list of the kings of the land that Joshua and the Israelites conquered on the west side of the Jordan, from Baal Gad in the Valley of Lebanon to Mount Halak, which rises toward Seir. Joshua gave their lands as an inheritance to the tribes of Israel according to their tribal divisions. 8 The lands included the hill country, the western foothills, the Arabah, the mountain slopes, the wilderness and the Negev. These were the lands of the Hittites, Amorites, Canaanites, Perizzites, Hivites and Jebusites. These were the kings:*

[9] the king of Jericho	one
the king of Ai (near Bethel)	one
[10] the king of Jerusalem	one
the king of Hebron	one
[11] the king of Jarmuth	one
the king of Lachish	one
[12] the king of Eglon	one
the king of Gezer	one
[13] the king of Debir	one
the king of Geder	one
[14] the king of Hormah	one
the king of Arad	one
[15] the king of Libnah	one
the king of Adullam	one
[16] the king of Makkedah	one
the king of Bethel	one
[17] the king of Tappuah	one
the king of Hepher	one
[18] the king of Aphek	one
the king of Lasharon	one

[19] *the king of Madon*	*one*
the king of Hazor	*one*
[20] *the king of Shimron Meron*	*one*
the king of Akshaph	*one*
[21] *the king of Taanach*	*one*
the king of Megiddo	*one*
[22] *the king of Kedesh*	*one*
the king of Jokneam in Carmel	*one*
[23] *the king of Dor (in Naphoth Dor)*	*one*
the king of Goyim in Gilgal	*one*
[24] *the king of Tirzah*	*one*

thirty-one kings in all.

When I first started reading the Bible on the mobile app, if I had read an esoteric scripture like this one, I would have not seen any deeper meaning. But after listening to the Bible every day for 4 months, new deeper meanings began to leap off the page. As I heard the name of each King Joshua defeated, followed by the repetitive word "one" after each and then hearing "thirty-one kings in all" at the end, a deeper meaning leapt from the scripture. I realized that the "one" was similar to the day-by-day approach to physical and mental health, and the total of kings was thirty-one, representing the days of the month. It came to me that "there is a king for every day of the month, and they must be defeated one by one and one day at a time."

In fact, I saw an aerial image of the human brain and began to see the wrinkles and creases of the brain like a geographical topography map with mountains and valleys. I pictured the brain divided into 31 land territories each occupied by an evil king. The process of reclaiming our mental land is a daily process of feeding all three dimensions of our human experiences. This in turn helps to defeat the evil king for each day and reclaim our mental land territory. I saw reclaiming my mental health as a game where I was defeating an evil king day by day. Then after 31 days, I would have defeated 31 Kings and reclaimed my mental health. From this daily Bible scripture reading was born 31 Kings Mental Health Game. This is the reason why this book is entitled 31 Kings...let's get ready for battle.

In the book <u>Battlefield of the Mind</u> by Joyce Meyer the author writes,

> God's word teaches us that our mind must be renewed so we learn to think like God thinks. When we do, then we can enjoy the life that God wants us to have—one of freedom, fruitfulness, peace, and joy. A whole new world opens up when we learn to <u>choose our own thoughts </u>rather than letting the devil fill our minds full of things that will destroy us. We must learn to be responsible for our thoughts and words because they produce our actions. It is impossible for us to behave better unless we think better thoughts[28]

---

[28] Meyer, J. (2008). *Battlefield of the mind: Winning the battle in your mind*. FaithWords.

Panic

When the fear is too great the reasoning mind begins to fail and we call this mental illness[29] (Ruiz, 2011)

I reflect on a hot and muggy pandemic morning in August 2020. I'm digging a hole to install a mailbox at our recently purchased land lot where we are building a glamping retreat center. I can feel the eyes of my new white neighbors. The night prior, the same neighbors called the police on me for being a Black man trespassing on my own land. I had to show the white male police officer my deed and matching driver license to prove my land ownership. After two days of manual labor and clearing the land by hand with a friend, my body was exhausted and dehydrated. I was not eating right, sleeping properly, or thinking about the positive promises of God. I went to sleep on my cousin's couch in a nearby apartment. Right before I fell asleep, I was watching CNN breaking news. CNN was repeatedly showing a violent police officer shooting a Black male. It was Jacob Blake being shot in the back by a white male Kenosha Wisconsin police officer. Then as I'm in that mental state between sleep and wake, I heard the news announcing the death of actor Chadwick Boseman who starred as The Black Panther, Jackie Robisnon, Thurgood Marshall, and so many powerful depictions of positive Black masculinity. Chadwick Boseman was the visual representation of Black manhood on screen, a once in a generation actor.

---

[29] Ruiz, D. M., & Mills, J. (2011). *The Four Agreements (Illustrated Edition): A Practical Guide to Personal Freedom (Four-color Illustrated Ed.).* Hay House, Inc.

So mentally I went to sleep watching a Black man shot in the back five times by a white police officer and also learned about the death of 'on screen' Black manhood. All this was the same day I was personally confronted by a white male police officer on my newly purchased land near majority white neighbors, who seemed to not be happy about my land purchase and appeared to want to intimidate or harm me. I felt like the days were running together.

As I was digging alone the next morning, I could feel my heart rate speeding up, my breath getting short, my mind racing with images of Black men being killed by white mobs, images of Emit Till at the museum in DC, images of the movie Rosewood (where an entire black town was massacred by jealous whites), images of the Wilmington, NC race riot, images of the Tulsa race massacre, images of politicians firing up white crowds saying 'outsiders!' (code for black people who are moving in and ruining suburban neighborhoods). I got light-headed and felt like I was going to faint. So I went and sat in my car and called my wife. It was while I was trying to explain to my wife, who is a therapist, what was going on with me that I realized I was having a panic attack. For the first time in my 40+ years on earth, I felt like my mind was working against me. Fear had gripped me in a way I had never experienced before and out of this experience grew a compassion for others who have been gripped by fear. That day I gained a deeper understanding of how other people feared me as a Black male. I learned how this fear encourages intimidation and manifests in acts of hate, racism, and violence. In the book The Four Agreements, the author writes, "when the fear is too great the reasoning mind begins to fail and we call this mental illness[30] (Ruiz, 2011)." For me, when I experienced mental illness and panic, it was because my lifestyle of burnout set my mind up to be filled with great fear. I let fear occupy the land of my mind. The solution for me is to adopt a mindset of a Daily Land Ownership approach to mental health, leading up to the development of the 31 Kings Mental Health Game.

Solution: Daily Land Ownership Paradigm

I said, "five in the morning" I wake up to fight for my earnings. The fear in my mind is a warning. Praying to the one you rely in. I've been wandering all day. I try to be fine but I can't be. The noise in my mind wouldn't leave me. I try to get by but I'm burning. And behind my mind it runs. All these thoughts have troubled me. Fighting to give up my pain. Fighting to be on my lane. My mind running to the other side. When it's time to live my life. Then it tries to take me out. Tell you what I need right here. I really need, I really need time now. I really need, I need a free mind now -Tims "Free Mind"

A Daily Land Ownership Mental Health Paradigm helped me to pay closer attention to two things:

1) Creating a **daily** mental, physical, and spiritual health routine which helped me to focus on winning the battle one day at a time

2) Looking at my mental health as **land ownership** gave me the understanding that ultimately I own the deed to

---

[30] Ruiz, D. M., & Mills, J. (2011). *The Four Agreements (Illustrated Edition): A Practical Guide to Personal Freedom (Four-color Illustrated Ed.).* Hay House, Inc.

my mental space and I can reclaim land that has been occupied by other thoughts.

First: Create a <u>Daily</u> Mental, Physical, and Spiritual Health Routine

Understanding that mental health is intimately connected to physical and spiritual health, it is important not to battle the mental trials of the past or tomorrow like a long-lasting war that spans for days and months. But instead, looking at the mental battlefield as a daily small battle is more beneficial and manageable. Think of it as "give us this day our daily bread," the focus is on seizing 'this' day. It is a "daily" view of life and life challenges. This requires a mental paradigm shift from worrying about tomorrow and/or re-living the traumatic thoughts, comments, or experiences of the past (without them being grounded in a purposeful use for today's battle). One of the mental health challenges that arose from the 2020 quarantine and isolation was the rapid pace in which so many Americans' lives slowed down. This can make the days feel like they are running together. The cause of this experience was defined by Segen's Medical Dictionary as *Boreout*[31]:

> 'A condition' that affects those who have too little work or lack stimulation from their jobs. Rather than being pleased with the abundant free time, bored workers grow disinterested, exhausted and even depressed. It is the flip side of burnout with the same symptoms.'

---

[31] Boreout. (n.d.) *Segen's Medical Dictionary.* (2011). Retrieved July 27 2022 from https://medical-dictionary.thefreedictionary.com/Boreout

By creating daily mental, physical, and spiritual health routines, it helps the mind to remain stimulated in times of quarantine and isolation. The 31 Kings Mental Health Game allows the user to set their own daily lifestyle goals and defeat the evil king through healthy lifestyle choices.

Second: Look at Mental Health as Land Ownership

The understanding that you ultimately have the deed to your own mental landscape is crucial for the second component of the Daily Land Ownership Mental Health Paradigm. If you look at an aerial view of the brian it looks like the typography of land.

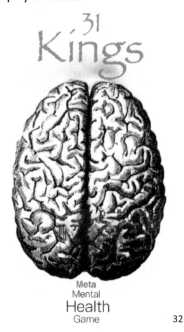

Meta
Mental
Health
Game   32

This visual understanding of our brain can help us approach our "mental space" or "attention" as a land asset that we sell or retain everyday through our activities,

---

[32] Brain artwork by Daniel Datiles

music, books, TV, news, and of course social media we voluntarily consume with our minds.

With these two new concepts in mind, we take a **Daily Land Ownership** approach to mental health. In 31 Kings, the user has a Daily Lifestyle Routine on each of the 31 days of the month. As the user completes each daily set of routines, they defeat the opposing king and retain their land ownership and kingdom for each day. At the end of 31 days, the user has now developed daily lifestyle routines that become a daily living habit that is natural and automatic for the user. Now the user no longer needs the game because they are winning in the game of life.

Game Time 31 Kings

Daily Lifestyle Game Calendar

The following calendar describes the day, word of the day and daily award for playing the 31 Kings Game. This calendar walks the user through the daily game found in the Purpose University Mobile app and 31 Kings online course.

Day	Word of the Day	Award for defeating King
Day 1	**Truth** **Body** -Exercise ☐ -Diet/Gut ☐ **Mind** -Meditate ☐ -Read ☐ **Spirit** -Prayer ☐ -Message ☐	Belt
Day 2	**Right** **Body** -Exercise ☐ -Diet/Gut ☐ **Mind** -Meditate ☐ -Read ☐ **Spirit** -Prayer ☐ -Message ☐	Breastplate
Day 3	**Peace** **Body** -Exercise ☐ -Diet/Gut ☐ **Mind** -Meditate ☐ -Read ☐ **Spirit** -Prayer ☐ -Message ☐	Feet Protection
Day 4	**Faith** **Body** -Exercise ☐	Shield

	-Diet/Gut ☐ **Mind** -Meditate ☐ -Read ☐ **Spirit** -Prayer ☐ -Message ☐	
Day 5	**Saved** **Body** **-**Exercise ☐ -Diet/Gut ☐ **Mind** -Meditate ☐ -Read ☐ **Spirit** -Prayer ☐ -Message ☐	**Helmet**
Day 6	**Word** **Body** **-**Exercise ☐ -Diet/Gut ☐ **Mind** -Meditate ☐ -Read ☐ **Spirit** -Prayer ☐ -Message ☐	**Sword**
Day 7	**REST**	
Day 8	**Pray** **Body** -Exercise ☐ -Diet/Gut ☐ **Mind** -Meditate ☐ -Read ☐ **Spirit** -Prayer ☐	**Add glow to Belt**

	-Message ☐	
Day 9	**People** **Body** -Exercise ☐ -Diet/Gut ☐ **Mind** -Meditate ☐ -Read ☐ **Spirit** -Prayer ☐ -Message ☐	**Add glow to Breastplate**
Day 10	**Pain** **Body** -Exercise ☐ -Diet/Gut ☐ **Mind** -Meditate ☐ -Read ☐ **Spirit** -Prayer ☐ -Message ☐	**Add glow to Feet**
Day 11	**Peace** **Body** -Exercise ☐ -Diet/Gut ☐ **Mind** -Meditate ☐ -Read ☐ **Spirit** -Prayer ☐ -Message ☐	**Add glow to Shield**
Day 12	**Passion** **Body** -Exercise ☐ -Diet/Gut ☐ **Mind** -Meditate ☐	**Add glow to Sword**

	-Read ☐ **Spirit** -Prayer ☐ -Message ☐	
Day 13	**Purpose** **Body** -Exercise ☐ -Diet/Gut ☐ **Mind** -Meditate ☐ -Read ☐ **Spirit** -Prayer ☐ -Message ☐	**Chair to think**
Day 14	**REST**	
Day 15	**Forgive** **Body** -Exercise ☐ -Diet/Gut ☐ **Mind** -Meditate ☐ -Read ☐ **Spirit** -Prayer ☐ -Message ☐	**Robe**
Day 15	**Release** **Body** -Exercise ☐ -Diet/Gut ☐ **Mind** -Meditate ☐ -Read ☐ **Spirit** -Prayer ☐ -Message ☐	**Ring**
Day 16	**Stop** **Body**	**Copper water Jug**

	-Exercise ☐ -Diet/Gut ☐ **Mind** -Meditate ☐ -Read ☐ **Spirit** -Prayer ☐ -Message ☐	
Day 17	**Still** **Body** -Exercise ☐ -Diet/Gut ☐ **Mind** -Meditate ☐ -Read ☐ **Spirit** -Prayer ☐ -Message ☐	**Fruit Smoothie**
Day 18	**Whole** **Body** -Exercise ☐ -Diet/Gut ☐ **Mind** -Meditate ☐ -Read ☐ **Spirit** -Prayer ☐ -Message ☐	**Apple Cider Vinegar glass of water**
Day 19	**Joy** **Body** -Exercise ☐ -Diet/Gut ☐ **Mind** -Meditate ☐ -Read ☐ **Spirit** -Prayer ☐ -Message ☐	**Vegetable boost**

Day 20	**Calm** **Body** -Exercise ☐ -Diet/Gut ☐ **Mind** -Meditate ☐ -Read ☐ **Spirit** -Prayer ☐ -Message ☐		**Fruit power boost**
Day 21	REST		**Trip the Beach/Nature**
Day 22	**Grounded** **Body** -Exercise ☐ -Diet/Gut ☐ **Mind** -Meditate ☐ -Read ☐ **Spirit** -Prayer ☐ -Message ☐		**Organic Garden**
Day 23	**Solid** **Body** -Exercise ☐ -Diet/Gut ☐ **Mind** -Meditate ☐ -Read ☐ **Spirit** -Prayer ☐ -Message ☐		**Organic Foods**
Day 24	**Relax** **Body** -Exercise ☐ -Diet/Gut ☐ **Mind** -Meditate ☐ -Read ☐		**Flowers in Garden**

	Spirit -Prayer ☐ -Message ☐	
Day 25	**Abundance** **Body** -Exercise ☐ -Diet/Gut ☐ **Mind** -Meditate ☐ -Read ☐ **Spirit** -Prayer ☐ -Message ☐	**Peaceful insects teaming the garden**
Day 26	**Hope** **Body** -Exercise ☐ -Diet/Gut ☐ **Mind** -Meditate ☐ -Read ☐ **Spirit** -Prayer ☐ -Message ☐	**Rain for the Garden**
Day 27	**Health** **Body** -Exercise ☐ -Diet/Gut ☐ **Mind** -Meditate ☐ -Read ☐ **Spirit** -Prayer ☐ -Message ☐	**Peaceful animals around garden**
Day 28	**REST**	**Friends come over for cookout**
Day 29	**Be** **Body** -Exercise ☐	**Meditation deck**

	-Diet/Gut ☐ **Mind** -Meditate ☐ -Read ☐ **Spirit** -Prayer ☐ -Message ☐	
Day 30	**Lean-in** **Body** -Exercise ☐ -Diet/Gut ☐ **Mind** -Meditate ☐ -Read ☐ **Spirit** -Prayer ☐ -Message ☐	**Improved hearing**
Day 31	**Love** **Body** -Exercise ☐ -Diet/Gut ☐ **Mind** -Meditate ☐ -Read ☐ **Spirit** -Prayer ☐ -Message ☐	**Fun time with kids in your family**

Closing Thoughts

Hopefully by now the reader understands why the book is not titled "Keep Going", "Reclaiming my Mind" or "Think on True Things", but all these elements can be found in the 31 Kings Mental Health Game. Everyday when we give, serve, teach, counsel, work, etc. This makes us positioned as "the helper". When we are the "helper" we are less likely to ask for "help".

For some of us, like me, we start a healthy mental health practice like meditation, prayer, therapy, or drinking apple cider vinegar and then lack another person to encourage us daily to "keep going".   In this book and game, it is my hope that the "helpers" use 31 Kings to develop their own mental health game to self-motivate and to "keep going!"

*Online Video Content

Wait it's not over! by purchasing this book you also gain access to the online daily video content. Download the Purpose University mobile App or go to **learnpurpose.teachable.com** use coupon code: DAILY to find:

Made in the USA
Middletown, DE
17 September 2023

38445297R00046